All Day Long

A Book of Partner Prayers

Deb Lund

illustrated by Carolyn Digby Conahan

MOREHOUSE PUBLISHING

A Continuum imprint

HARRISBURG · LONDON · NEW YORK

Morehouse Publishing
A Continuum Imprint

4775 Linglestown Road
Harrisburg, PA 17112

The Tower Building
11 York Road
London SE1 7NX

Cover design by Brenda Klinger

Library of Congress Cataloging-in-Publication Data

Lund, Deb.
  All day long : a book of partner prayers / Deb Lund ; illustrated by
Carolyn Digby Conahan.
      p. cm.
  ISBN 0-8192-1961-4 (hardcover)
  1. Christian children--Prayer-books and devotions--English. [1.
Prayers.] I. Conahan, Carolyn, ill. II. Title.
  BV4870.L86 2004
  242'.82--dc22
                                        2003023311

Printed in Malaysia

04 05 06 07 08 09   10 9 8 7 6 5 4 3 2 1

For the Clausens,

our all-day-long friends

Partner prayers are meant to be shared.
Repeated responses make these prayer-poems
interactive and accessible for even the very young.

Waking Up

I wake up, stretch, and wiggle toes,
Thank you for this day!

I blink and yawn, then scratch my nose,
Thank you for this day!

I hope it's all that it can be,
Thank you for this day!

This brand new day of being me.
Thank you for this day!

*Those who believe each day is
special honor and give thanks
to God. —Romans 14:6*

Breakfast

I've got milk, a banana, a bowl, and a spoon.
  Bless all who brought us this food.

I'll be eating my favorite cereal soon.
  Bless all who brought us this food.

Whether it's juice and some toast smeared with jam.
  Bless all who brought us this food.

Or a big pile of pancakes with fried eggs and ham.
  Bless all who brought us this food.

*You and your family will eat with
God, thankful for your blessings.
—Deuteronomy 12:7*

Getting Dressed

I fold my pajamas, then put them away.
God is here beside me.

I think I'll wear pants and a T-shirt today.
God is here beside me.

My socks get all twisted, I tug them up so.
God is here beside me.

Then on go my shoes and I'm ready to go.
God is here beside me.

*...May God's steadfast love and
faithfulness watch over you.*
—Psalm 61:7

Learning

Quarter, penny, nickel, dime,
Counting, adding, telling time.
Thanks for all I'm learning.

Paint a picture, read a book,
Find a recipe to cook.
Thanks for all I'm learning.

Tell a story, sing a song,
I can learn things all day long.
Thanks for all I'm learning.

Let the wise listen and learn...
—Proverbs 1:5

Playing with Friends

I play soccer with Susie and T-ball with Ben.
God is smiling as we play.

We all like to play hide-and-seek now and then.
God is smiling as we play.

We dig for lost treasure and put on a play,
God is smiling as we play.

And God is here watching us all through the day.
God is smiling as we play.

Dear Friend, since God loves
us so much, we should love
each other. —1 John 4:11

At Home

At times it's no fun putting playthings away,
Or cleaning my room when my mom and dad say.
Thanks for all I have.

They say, "Clear off the table" and "Go feed the cat."
I wish that they wouldn't be bossy like that.
Thanks for all I have.

But when I get crabby and hear myself whine,
I say all my thank-yous, and then I feel fine.
Thanks for all I have.

We have food and a home, and we all do our best,
And knowing God loves us makes up for the rest.
Thanks for all I have.

Everything made by God is good if
we are thankful when we receive it.
— 1 Timothy 4:4

Quiet Time

Painting, reading, writing, dreaming.
   Quiet time with God.

Praying, sighing, wishing, flying.
   Quiet time with God.

Thanking, thinking, sharing, singing.
   Quiet time with God.

Growing, giving, loving, living.
   Quiet time with God.

It is good to wait quietly for
God. —Lamentations 3:26

Dinner

I hold out my paws as I sit in my chair.
  Bless this food and family.

They don't seem to know I'm a big hungry bear.
  Bless this food and family.

I could gobble them up, but I think I'll behave.
  Bless this food and family.

This circle of hands makes a warm cozy cave.
Bless this food and family.

*With a strong hand and
outstretched arm, God's love
is forever. —Psalm 136:12*

Evening

You were loved before your birth,
No matter where you live on earth.
Help us remember each other.

You might not eat the snacks I like,
Or look like me or ride a bike.
Help us remember each other.

And though I might not meet you soon,
I bounce a wish right off the moon.
Help us remember each other.

May your days be free from fear,
And may you know that God is near.
Help us remember each other.

...Love your neighbor as yourself.
—Luke 10:27

Bedtime

Now it's my bath time. So where is my duck?
Right here the whole time.

I can't find my PJs. Would you try your luck?
Right here the whole time.

My teeth are all brushed. So now where is my book?
Right here the whole time.

Did you see my blanket? Oh, please help me look!
Right here the whole time.

Where are you, Bear, with your wink and a song?
Right here the whole time.

So, tell me now, God, where were YOU all day long?
Right here the whole time.

Where can I go from your spirit?
Wherever I go, you are there.
—Psalm 139:7–8

Deb Lund is the author of *Play & Pray*, *Me & God*, *Dinosailors*, and *Tell Me My Story, Mama*. She is a classroom and music teacher and librarian. Deb co-directs a homeschool support program and teaches writing classes for children and teachers. She visits schools and libraries as an author and as a member of the Basics, a children's music group. Deb lives on an island in Puget Sound with her husband Karl and son Kaj. You may contact Deb or learn more about her at www.DebLund.com.

Carolyn Digby Conahan studied at Reed College and the Pacific Northwest College of Art. Her illustrations have appeared in a variety of publications for children and adults. Currently, she is the staff illustrator for *Cricket* magazine. She lives with her husband, children, one grandma, two cats, and a dog in Oregon.